Made With Love For

_____

By

_____

LUXURY FAMILY
PRESS

Family Tree

childhood

What do you remember the most about your childhood?

What's one of your favorite memories from childhood?

What is your earliest memory?

What is your full name and why were you named that? Did you have a nickname?

_____
_____
_____
_____
_____
_____
_____
_____
_____
_____
_____
_____
_____
_____
_____
_____
_____
_____
_____
_____
_____
_____
_____
_____
_____

What was your hometown like (where you grew up)?

What was your favorite toy or activity as a child?

What was one of your favorite shows as a child?

_____
_____
_____
_____
_____
_____
_____
_____
_____
_____
_____
_____
_____
_____
_____
_____
_____
_____
_____
_____
_____
_____
_____

What was your prized possession as a kid?

_____
_____
_____
_____
_____
_____
_____
_____
_____
_____
_____
_____
_____
_____
_____
_____
_____
_____
_____
_____
_____
_____

What were you most proud of as a kid?

_____
_____
_____
_____
_____
_____
_____
_____
_____
_____
_____
_____
_____
_____
_____
_____
_____
_____
_____
_____
_____
_____
_____

Were you ever bored as a child? Who was your best friend as a child?

_____

_____

_____

_____

_____

_____

_____

_____

_____

_____

_____

_____

_____

_____

_____

_____

_____

_____

_____

_____

_____

_____

_____

What did you love doing as a kid?

What was your favorite pet when you were a kid?

_____
_____
_____
_____
_____
_____
_____
_____
_____
_____
_____
_____
_____
_____
_____
_____
_____
_____
_____
_____
_____

What did you get in trouble for when you were a kid?

_____

_____

_____

_____

_____

_____

_____

_____

_____

_____

_____

_____

_____

_____

_____

_____

_____

_____

_____

_____

_____

_____

Did you ever have a teacher who picked on you?

What special kinds of food did your
mother give you when you sick?
Why did she give you those foods?

_____
_____
_____
_____
_____
_____
_____
_____
_____
_____
_____
_____
_____
_____
_____
_____
_____
_____
_____
_____
_____
_____
_____
_____
_____
_____

When you were young, did you collect anything? If you did, what was it and why did you get into that?

_____

_____

_____

_____

_____

_____

_____

_____

_____

_____

_____

_____

_____

_____

_____

_____

_____

_____

_____

_____

_____

What did you want to be when you grew up?

School

How would people who knew you in high school describe you?

_____

_____

_____

_____

_____

_____

_____

_____

_____

_____

_____

_____

_____

_____

_____

_____

_____

_____

_____

_____

How would people who knew you in middle school describe you then?

Who was your favorite teacher at school?

Were you considered popular in middle school or high school? Why or why not?

What was your most important relationship in high school and why did it end?

_____
_____
_____
_____
_____
_____
_____
_____
_____
_____
_____
_____
_____
_____
_____
_____
_____
_____
_____
_____
_____
_____
_____
_____
_____

Who was your best friend in high school and what was the best thing about this person?

When you were in high school, what did you want to be when you grew up? What about college? How did you come up with those ideas?

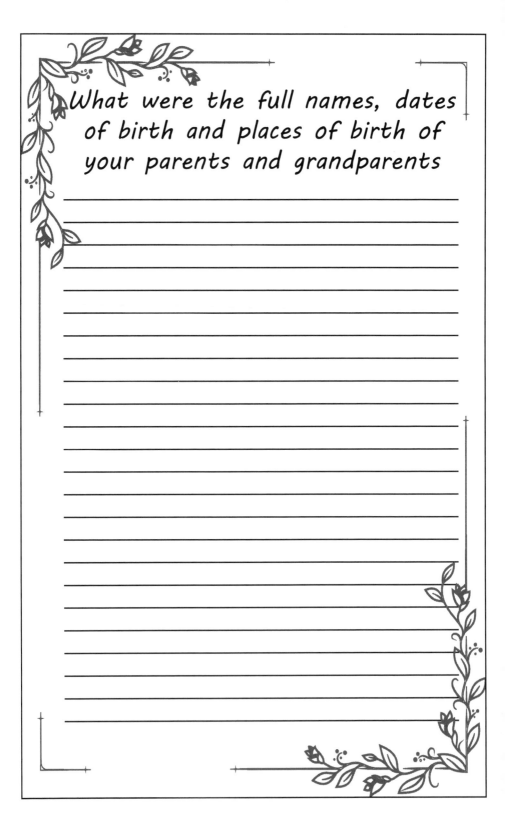

What were the full names, dates of birth and places of birth of your parents and grandparents

What do you remember most about your mother?

What do you remember most about your father?

_____
_____
_____
_____
_____
_____
_____
_____
_____
_____
_____
_____
_____
_____
_____
_____
_____
_____
_____
_____
_____
_____

What do you remember most about your grandparents?

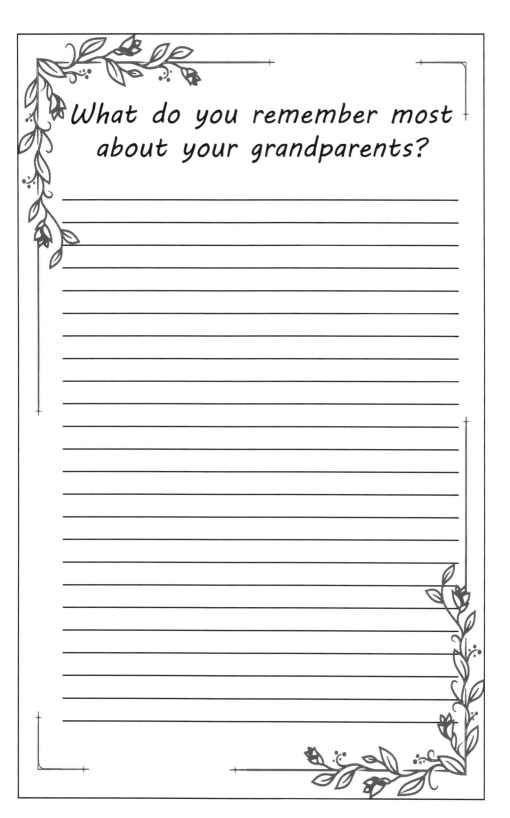

Are there any other family members you particularly remember? What makes them stand out in your mind?

_____

_____

_____

_____

_____

_____

_____

_____

_____

_____

_____

_____

_____

_____

_____

_____

_____

_____

_____

_____

_____

_____

_____

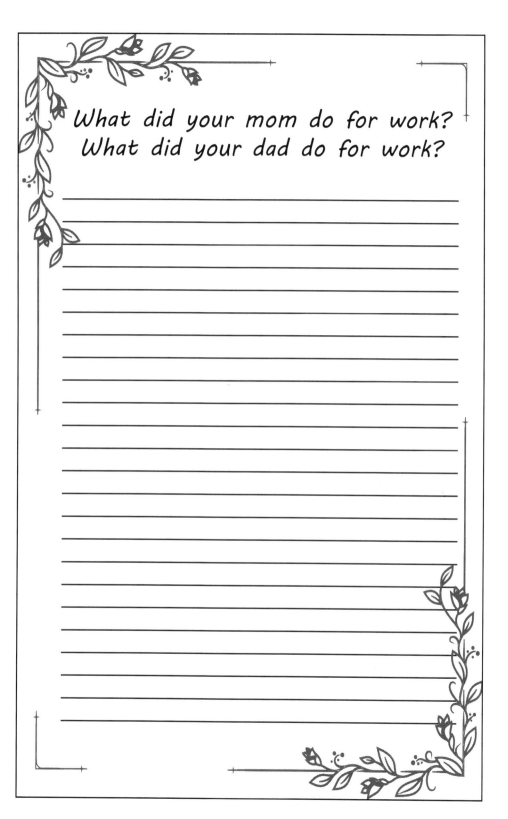

What did your mom do for work?
What did your dad do for work?

_____
_____
_____
_____
_____
_____
_____
_____
_____
_____
_____
_____
_____
_____
_____
_____
_____
_____
_____
_____
_____
_____
_____

Tell me about your brothers and sisters.

What was your home life like? What did your home look like?

_____

_____

_____

_____

_____

_____

_____

_____

_____

_____

_____

_____

_____

_____

_____

_____

_____

_____

_____

_____

_____

_____

How did you and Mom/Dad meet?

Who were your parents?
Who were your grandparents?
Where are they from?

What are your favorite family recipes? How do we get them?

_____

_____

_____

_____

_____

_____

_____

_____

_____

_____

_____

_____

_____

_____

_____

_____

_____

_____

_____

_____

_____

_____

Did your family have money growing up?

How old were your parents when they died?
How old were your grandparents when they died?

What did your parents and grandparents die from?

How would you describe Dad/ Mom the first time you saw him/her?

What is the worst thing that your parents ever said to you?

_____

_____

_____

_____

_____

_____

_____

_____

_____

_____

_____

_____

_____

_____

_____

_____

_____

_____

_____

_____

Who was more strict when you were growing up, your mother or father? How did you feel about that?

_____

_____

_____

_____

_____

_____

_____

_____

_____

_____

_____

_____

_____

_____

_____

_____

_____

_____

_____

_____

_____

What was your relationship with your own parents like?

What do I need to know about our family's medical history that could affect my health or life?

How many children were in your family? What are there full names?

Could you tell me a story or a special memory about your brothers and sisters?

_____

_____

_____

_____

_____

_____

_____

_____

_____

_____

_____

_____

_____

_____

_____

_____

_____

_____

_____

_____

_____

_____

_____

What is something special that happened to you?

What is something terrible that happened to you?

Pick three words to describe your personality.

What would you think are the great inventions in your lifetime?

What is something I still might not know about you?

What do you wish you had more time for in life?

If you could go back in time and change one thing what would it be?

Did you ever do anything naughty/mischievous?

_____

_____

_____

_____

_____

_____

_____

_____

_____

_____

_____

_____

_____

_____

_____

_____

_____

_____

_____

_____

_____

Did you ever have your heart broken?

Were you ever scared of anything?

What are the most important lessons you have learned over time?

_____
_____
_____
_____
_____
_____
_____
_____
_____
_____
_____
_____
_____
_____
_____
_____
_____
_____
_____
_____
_____
_____
_____
_____
_____

Has anyone ever disappointed you?

Has anyone ever hurt you?

What is the most thankful gift in your life??

_____
_____
_____
_____
_____
_____
_____
_____
_____
_____
_____
_____
_____
_____
_____
_____
_____
_____
_____
_____

Who has inspired you the most in life?

How has society and the world changed since you were young?

Describe the day you started your first job

What do you love doing now?

Have you ever met anyone famous?

_____

_____

_____

_____

_____

_____

_____

_____

_____

_____

_____

_____

_____

_____

_____

_____

_____

_____

_____

_____

What was the first house you ever bought?

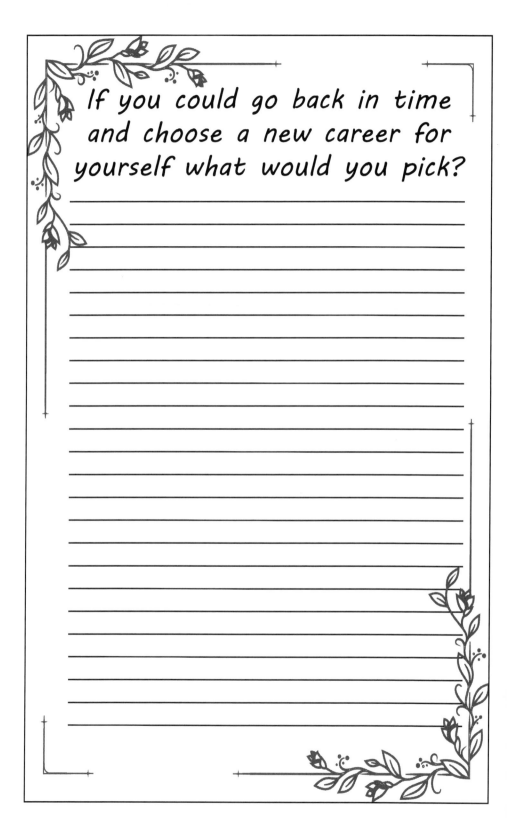

If you could go back in time and choose a new career for yourself what would you pick?

What have you always been good at?

What is the hardest thing you have ever done?

What is the best thing you have ever done?

_____

_____

_____

_____

_____

_____

_____

_____

_____

_____

_____

_____

_____

_____

_____

_____

_____

_____

_____

What do you miss most about the" good old days?"

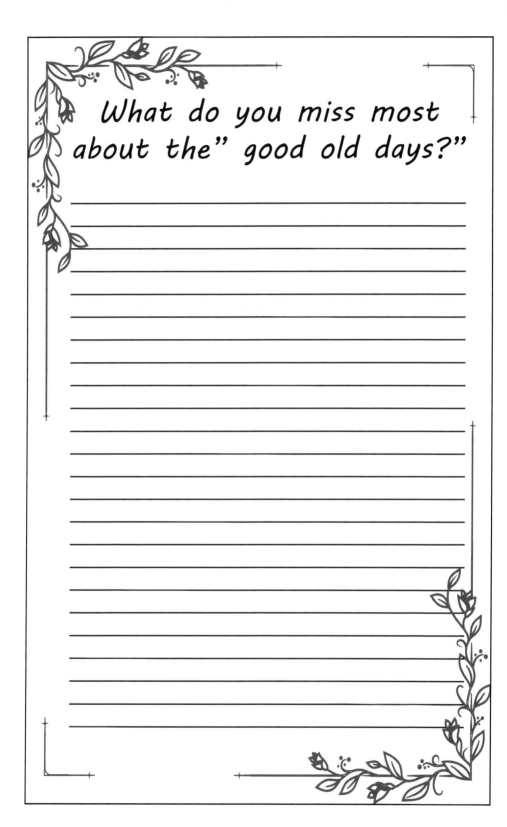

How much was your first paycheck?

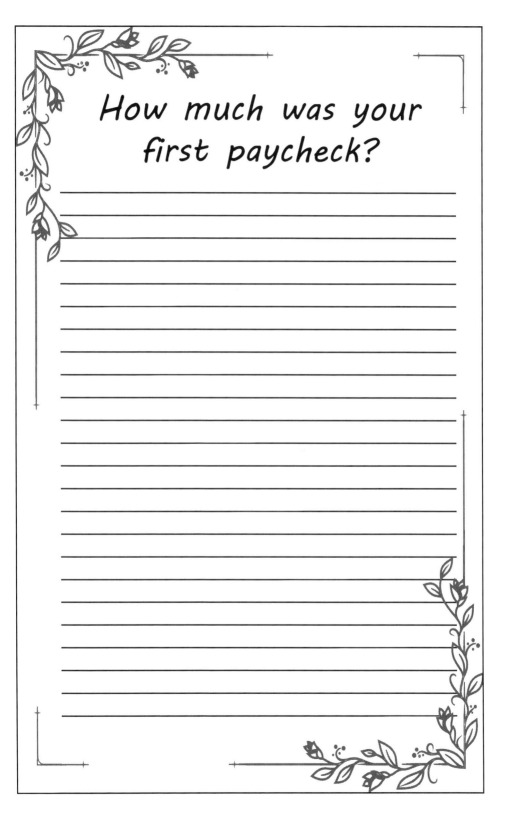

Where did you go on your honeymoon?

How did you celebrate your birthdays?

_____
_____
_____
_____
_____
_____
_____
_____
_____
_____
_____
_____
_____
_____
_____
_____
_____
_____
_____
_____
_____

Which friends did you see most often?

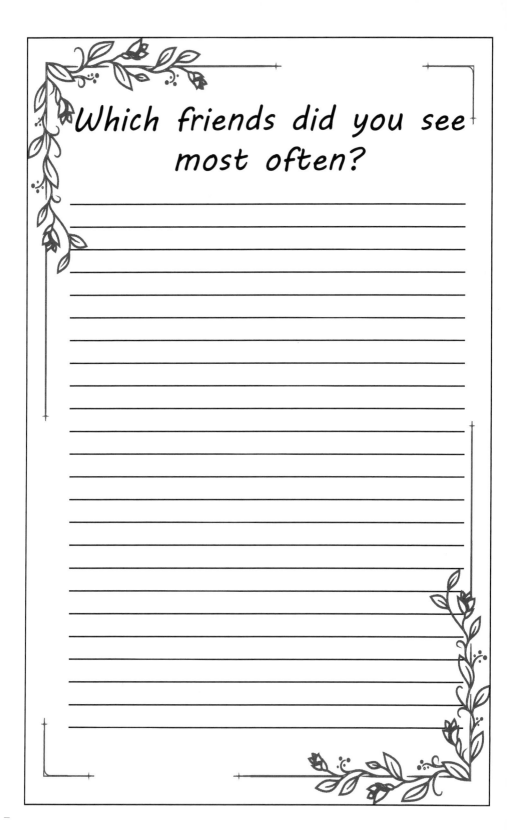

What is the best birthday present you ever got?

How many countries have you visited?

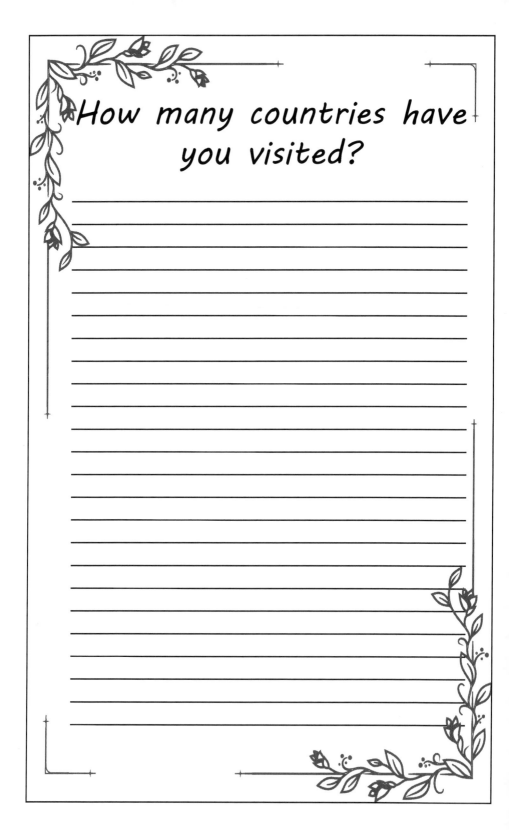

What is your favorite city in this world?

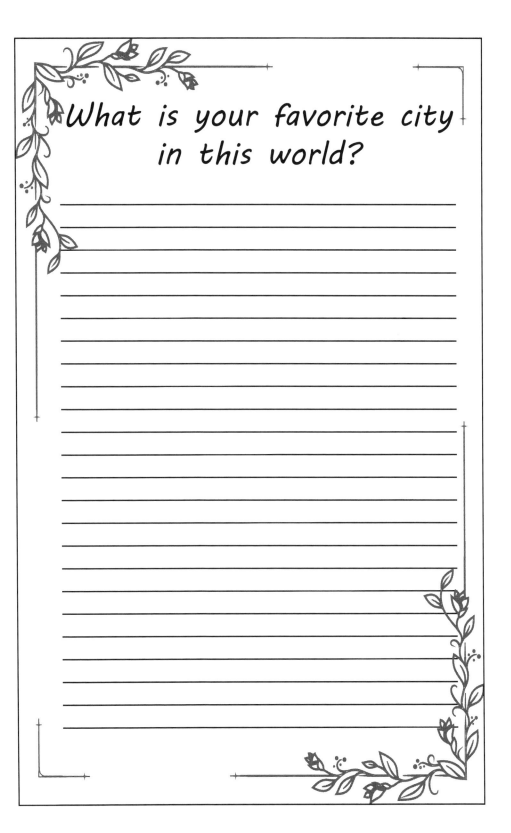

Why did you choose to live where you live now?

Did you ever have a pet?

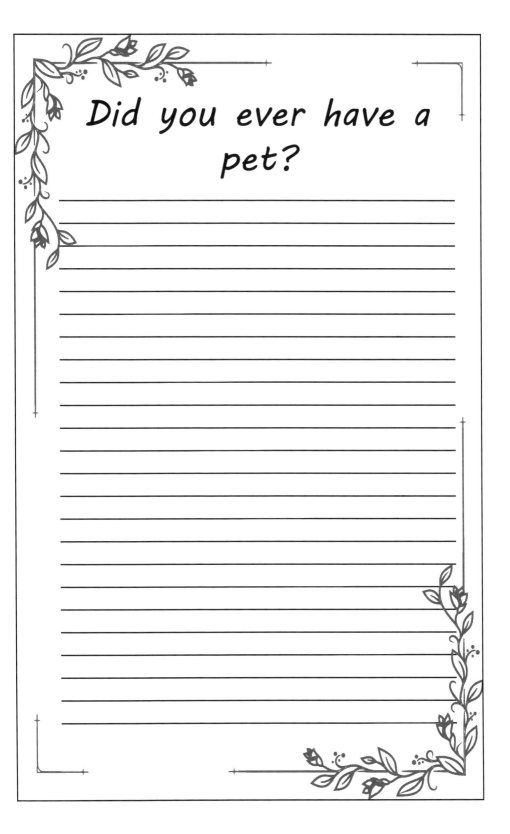

Is there any city/country you still wish you could visit?

_____
_____
_____
_____
_____
_____
_____
_____
_____
_____
_____
_____
_____
_____
_____
_____
_____
_____
_____
_____
_____
_____
_____
_____

Have you ever been the victim of a crime?

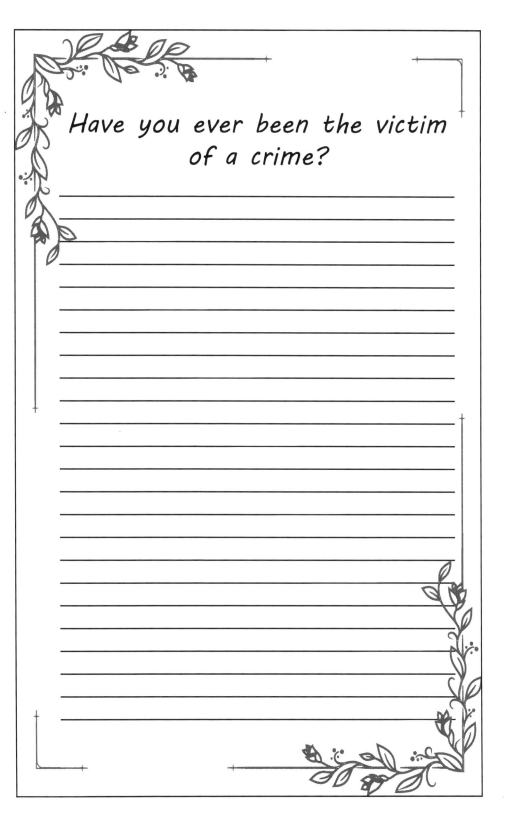

Have you been in a serious accident?

Did you ever do anything naughty/mischievous?

_____

_____

_____

_____

_____

_____

_____

_____

_____

_____

_____

_____

_____

_____

_____

_____

_____

_____

_____

Has anyone ever saved your life?

Have you ever made mistakes in life?

_____
_____
_____
_____
_____
_____
_____
_____
_____
_____
_____
_____
_____
_____
_____
_____
_____
_____
_____
_____
_____
_____

What have you learned from these mistakes?

What are your hobbies?

What is the most beautiful place you have ever visited and what was it like?

_____
_____
_____
_____
_____
_____
_____
_____
_____
_____
_____
_____
_____
_____
_____
_____
_____
_____
_____
_____
_____
_____
_____
_____

What states have you visited? What countries have you visited?

What pets have you had? Tell me about them.

_____

_____

_____

_____

_____

_____

_____

_____

_____

_____

_____

_____

_____

_____

_____

_____

_____

_____

_____

_____

_____

_____

Is there anything you have always wanted to do but haven't?

_____

_____

_____

_____

_____

_____

_____

_____

_____

_____

_____

_____

_____

_____

_____

_____

_____

_____

_____

_____

Do you think money can buy you happiness?

_____
_____
_____
_____
_____
_____
_____
_____
_____
_____
_____
_____
_____
_____
_____
_____
_____
_____
_____
_____
_____
_____

What advice would you give to your younger self?

_____

_____

_____

_____

_____

_____

_____

_____

_____

_____

_____

_____

_____

_____

_____

_____

_____

_____

_____

_____

_____

_____

What makes you happy?

What makes you sad?
What makes you angry?

What makes you feel loved?

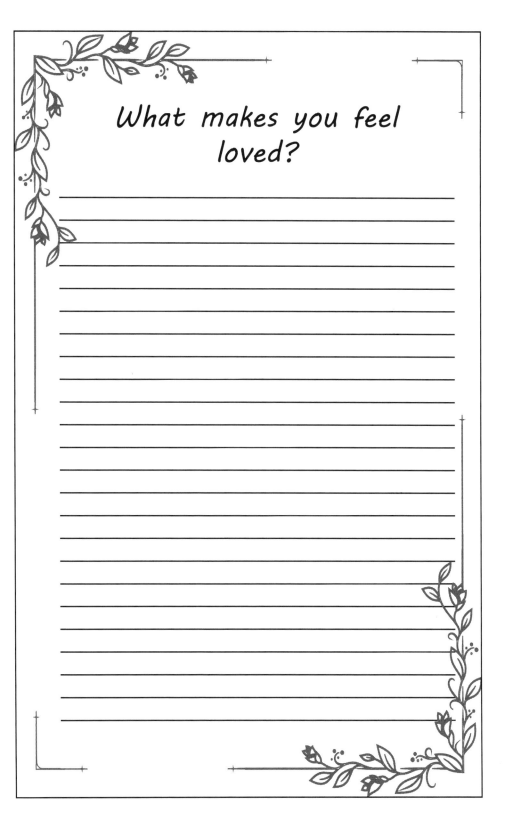

Do you believe in love at first sight?

If you could invite 5 famous people to dinner who would you invite?

_____
_____
_____
_____
_____
_____
_____
_____
_____
_____
_____
_____
_____
_____
_____
_____
_____
_____
_____
_____
_____
_____
_____
_____

If you could be invisible for a day, what would you do?

_____
_____
_____
_____
_____
_____
_____
_____
_____
_____
_____
_____
_____
_____
_____
_____
_____
_____
_____
_____
_____
_____

When, if ever, do you think it's okay to tell a lie?

What was the best thing I ever gave you?

Do you think you have any prejudices? What would they be?

If a friend of yours told you that he
or she did something dishonest, would
you report him or her to the police?
Why or why not?

What kinds of scenes in movies make you cry?

Is there any experience that you have not had that you regret not having?

What makes a good friend?

Would you rather be famous, or make a lot of money? Why?

_____

_____

_____

_____

_____

_____

_____

_____

_____

_____

_____

_____

_____

_____

_____

_____

_____

_____

_____

_____

What is your biggest worry?

_____
_____
_____
_____
_____
_____
_____
_____
_____
_____
_____
_____
_____
_____
_____
_____
_____
_____
_____

What memories stick out most for you in life?

_____
_____
_____
_____
_____
_____
_____
_____
_____
_____
_____
_____
_____
_____
_____
_____
_____
_____
_____
_____
_____
_____

What advice would you give your -20year-old self?

What have you always wanted to ask me?

Made in the USA
Columbia, SC
14 December 2022

74023653R00067